KINGDOM AUTHORITY

LIVING UNDER GOD'S RULE

TONY EVANS

Lifeway Press®
Brentwood, Tennessee

EDITORIAL TEAM

Heather Hair
Writer

Tyler Quillet
Managing Editor

Reid Patton
Senior Editor

Joel Polk
Publisher, Small Group Publishing

Angel Prohaska
Associate Editor

Brian Daniel
Director, Adult Ministry Publishing

Jon Rodda
Art Director

Published by Lifeway Press® • © 2022 Tony Evans

ISBN: 978-1-0877-7742-9
Item number: 005840820

Dewey decimal classification: 248.84

Subject heading: CHRISTIAN LIFE \ PROVIDENCE AND GOVERNMENT OF GOD \ GOD-WILL

My deepest thanks go to Mrs. Heather Hair for her skills and insights in collaboration on this manuscript.

Unless indicated otherwise, Scripture quotations are taken from the New American Standard Bible®, Copyright © 1960, 1971, 1977, 1995, 2020 by The Lockman Foundation. Used by permission. All rights reserved. www.lockman.org.

To order additional copies of this resource, write to Lifeway Resources Customer Service; 200 Powell Place, Suite 100; Brentwood, TN, 37027; fax 615-251-5933; call toll free 800-458-2772; order online at *lifeway.com;* email *orderentry@lifeway.com.*

Printed in the United States of America

Adult Ministry Publishing • Lifeway Resources • 200 Powell Place, Suite 100 • Brentwood, TN 37027

Contents

WEEK 1

WEEK 2

WEEK 3

WEEK 4

WEEK 5

WEEK 6

About the Author

Dr. Tony Evans is the founder and senior pastor of Oak Cliff Bible Fellowship in Dallas, founder and president of The Urban Alternative, former chaplain of the NBA's Dallas Mavericks, and author of over 100 books, booklets, and Bible studies. The first African American to earn a doctorate of theology from Dallas Theological Seminary, he has been named one of the twelve most effective preachers in the English-speaking world by Baylor University. Dr. Evans holds the honor of writing and publishing the first full-Bible commentary and study Bible by an African American.

His radio broadcast, *The Alternative with Dr. Tony Evans*, can be heard on more than fourteen thousand US outlets daily and in more than 130 countries.

Dr. Evans launched the Tony Evans Training Center in 2017, an online learning platform providing quality seminary-style courses for a fraction of the cost to any person in any place. The goal is to increase Bible literacy not only in lay people but also in those Christian leaders who cannot afford nor find the time for formal ongoing education.

Dr. Tony Evans was married to his late wife, Lois, for nearly fifty years. They are the proud parents of four, grandparents of thirteen and great-grandparents of four.

For more information, visit TonyEvans.org.

HOW TO GET THE MOST FROM THIS STUDY

This Bible study book includes six weeks of
content for group and personal study.

GROUP SESSIONS

Regardless of what day of the week your group meets, each week of content begins with the group session. Each group session uses the following format to facilitate meaningful interaction among group members, with God's Word, and with the teaching of Dr. Evans.

START. This page includes questions to get the conversation started and to introduce the video teaching.

WATCH. This page includes key points from Dr. Evans's teaching, along with blanks for taking notes as participants watch the video.

DISCUSS. This page includes questions and statements that guide the group to respond to Dr. Evans's video teaching and to relevant Bible passages.

PERSONAL STUDY

Each week provides three days of Bible study and learning activities for individual engagement between group sessions: "Hit the Streets" and two Bible studies.

HIT THE STREETS. This section highlights practical steps for taking the week's teaching and putting it into practice.

BIBLE STUDIES. These personal studies revisit stories, Scriptures, and themes introduced in the videos in order to understand and apply them on a personal level.

TIPS FOR LEADING A SMALL GROUP

Follow these guidelines to prepare for each group session.

PRAYERFULLY PREPARE

REVIEW. Review the weekly material and group questions ahead of time.

PRAY. Be intentional about praying for each person in the group.

Ask the Holy Spirit to work through you and the group discussion as you point to Jesus each week through God's Word.

MINIMIZE DISTRACTIONS

Create a comfortable environment. If group members are uncomfortable, they'll be distracted and therefore not engaged in the group experience. Plan ahead by considering details like seating, temperature, lighting, food and drink, surrounding noise, and general cleanliness.

At best, thoughtfulness and hospitality show guests and group members they're welcome and valued in whatever environment you choose to gather. At worst, people may never notice your effort, but they're also not distracted. Do everything in your ability to help people focus on what's most important: connecting with God, with the Bible, and with one another.

INCLUDE OTHERS

Your goal is to foster a community in which people are welcome just as they are but encouraged to grow spiritually. Always be aware of opportunities to include any people who visit the group and to invite new people to join your group.

An inexpensive way to make first-time guests feel welcome or to invite someone to get involved is to give them their own copies of this Bible study book.

ENCOURAGE DISCUSSION
A good small group experience has the following characteristics.

EVERYONE PARTICIPATES. Encourage everyone to ask questions, share responses, or read aloud.

NO ONE DOMINATES—NOT EVEN THE LEADER. Be sure that your time speaking as a leader takes up less than half of your time together as a group. Politely guide discussion if anyone dominates.

NOBODY IS RUSHED THROUGH QUESTIONS. Don't feel that a moment of silence is a bad thing. People often need time to think about their responses to questions they've just heard or to gain courage to share what God is stirring in their hearts.

INPUT IS AFFIRMED AND FOLLOWED UP. Make sure you point out something true or helpful in a response. Don't just move on. Build community with follow-up questions, asking how other people have experienced similar things or how a truth has shaped their understanding of God and the Scripture you're studying. People are less likely to speak up if they fear that you don't actually want to hear their answers or that you're looking for only a certain answer.

GOD AND HIS WORD ARE CENTRAL. Opinions and experiences can be helpful, but God has given us the truth. Trust God's Word to be the authority and God's Spirit to work in people's lives. You can't change anyone, but God can. Continually point people to the Word and to active steps of faith.

KEEP CONNECTING

Think of ways to connect with group members during the week.

Participation during the group session is always improved when members spend time connecting with one another outside the group sessions. The more people are comfortable with and involved in one another's lives, the more they'll look forward to being together. When people move beyond being friendly to truly being friends who form a community, they come to each session eager to engage instead of merely attending.

Encourage group members with thoughts, commitments, or questions from the session by connecting through emails, texts and social media.

When possible, build deeper friendships by planning or spontaneously inviting group members to join you outside your regularly scheduled group time for meals, fun activities, or projects around your home, church, or community.

WEEK 1

THE CONCEPT OF KINGDOM AUTHORITY

Start

Welcome to group session 1.

Imagine trying to view your life through glasses that have never been cleaned. After years of wear and tear, you would have scratches, grime, and dust all over them. Imagine trying to drive with them on. Or even having a conversation with them on. Or watching a movie.

The videos for this study were filmed in Ireland, where everywhere you look is a more brilliant shade of green. The expansiveness of the scenery testified to God's great power and creative prowess. But if dirty glasses were obscuring your vision, you wouldn't be able to take it all in! The beauty would still be there, but you'd be incapable of fully appreciating it.

Why is it important to be able to see clearly
as you navigate your physical life?

Why is it important to be able to see clearly
as you navigate your spiritual life?

When we are unable to see clearly, it is difficult to know what steps to take or to recognize dangers ahead of us. Moving through life unimpeded often requires keen physical eyesight. But did you know that our spiritual eyesight is just as critical? In fact, spiritual eyesight is even more critical. Without a right spiritual perspective, we will not be able to see the truth and will miss out on recognizing how to access the kingdom authority which is ours to have. That's why Paul prayed in Ephesians 1:18 that our spiritual eyes (the eyes of our hearts) would be opened and enlightened.

As we start our study through the subject of kingdom authority, we must start with the eyes of our hearts. It's only when we see God for who He truly is that we can know how to align ourselves underneath His righteous rule and tap into the spiritual power we need to live a life of kingdom authority.

Ask someone to pray then watch group session 1.

Watch

Use this space to take notes on video session 1.

Discuss

Use the following questions to discuss the video teaching.

One of the primary things Paul wanted believers in Ephesus to see once the eyes of their hearts were opened was where they were standing—where they were located, spiritually. Paul tells us this in Ephesians 2:4-6:

> *But God, being rich in mercy, because of His great love with which He loved us,*
> *even when we were dead in our wrongdoings, made us alive together*
> *with Christ (by grace you have been saved), and raised us up with Him,*
> *and seated us with Him in the heavenly places in Christ Jesus.*
> EPHESIANS 2:4-6

It's easy to forget where you are when you cannot see. Have you ever had to open your eyes during a dream in order to figure out if you were in the dream or the safety of your own bed? That's okay when you are dreaming but it's not okay when you are trying to live your life with kingdom authority.

Share about a time when you got lost.
What did you learn through that experience?

What are some reasons it's important for believers to know
where they stand in relationship to God and His kingdom?

In the video, Dr. Evans talks to us from a very high place called the Cliffs of Moher in Ireland and it is one of the most scenic locations on the planet. These cliffs rise to just over seven hundred feet at their highest point. Paul wants us to realize where we are, sharpen our spiritual perspective, and to help us see that we are seated with Christ in the heavenly realm.

Jesus is on the seat of authority—the throne from which He
reigns. Why does it matter that we are seated there with Him?

How does it change your perspective to realize you're
seated with Christ on high in the heavenly places?

Dr. Evans set the stage for our study on kingdom authority by letting us know where the battles in life really take place. He taught that everything visible and physical is first preceded by something invisible and spiritual. So, if you want to address the visible, physical realm, you must understand, identify, and address the invisible, spiritual cause. Because if you miss the invisible, spiritual cause, you will not understand how to address the visible, physical realities. There is a spiritual realm of authority, and there is a battle that takes place in that realm.

Share a time you witnessed the invisible, spiritual
realm impacting your physical reality.

Dr. Evans defined kingdom authority as *the divinely delegated right and responsibility for believers to act on God's behalf in ruling His creation underneath the Lordship of Jesus Christ.*

Why do believers need to grab hold of and exercise this
God-given authority? What happens if we don't?

What are some practical steps we can take to engage
with God and develop our spiritual eyesight?

Let's end our Bible study time in prayer.

Prayer

Lord, in times that it becomes easy to see only that which is right
before our eyes, help us to see from Your vantage point instead.
Remind us that we are seated on high with You and need to view
all of life through a spiritual lens. In Jesus's name, amen.

HIT THE STREETS
Seeing the Spiritual

Have you ever noticed when you are in an airplane how small and orderly everything looks down below? That's because you are looking at it from way up. But when you land on the ground, chaos ensues as you enter traffic and try and find which way to go because you can't see the big picture.

Until you learn to exchange human wisdom for the big picture—divine wisdom —you'll stay stuck in the chaos, mess, and traffic jams of life. Whether it be personal traffic, familial traffic, circumstantial traffic, or any other, if you don't learn to view the routes and pathways of life from the vantage point of heaven, you won't be able to access the kingdom authority that rightfully belongs to you.

You start from where you're seated. Therefore, you must learn to view all of life from an authoritative kingdom perspective. When you learn to operate and make your decisions from where you are truly seated with Christ, you will access the authority you need to live out the fullness of God's plans.

Below are three key passages that describe the spiritual realm and how to access it. Read them slowly, then use the space provide to summarize them in your own words.

While we look not at the things which are seen, but at the things which are not seen; for the things which are seen are temporal, but the things which are not seen are eternal.
2 CORINTHIANS 4:18

Personal Summary:

Set your mind on the things that are above,
not on the things that are on earth.
COLOSSIANS 3:2

Personal Summary:

"For My thoughts are not your thoughts, nor are your ways My ways,"
declares the LORD. "For as the heavens are higher than the earth, so are
My ways higher than your ways and My thoughts than your thoughts."
ISAIAH 55:8-9

Personal Summary:

What is your primary takeaway from meditating on these truths?

BIBLE STUDY 1

The War for Authority

If you were to travel to Northern Ireland from one of the locations we visited to film this Bible study, you would literally be traveling to another country. In fact, you would even need to exchange your euros for pounds if you wanted to gas up your car or go to a restaurant or buy some souvenirs.

Even though they occupy the same island and the land may appear to be the same land to the average viewer other than the flags flying above them, the governments of Ireland and Northern Ireland are distinct. Ireland is an independent nation and Northern Ireland is a part of the United Kingdom and governed by the British. As a result, euros are not accepted currency in Northern Ireland, just as the British pound is not an accepted currency in the remaining parts of the island not governed by the brits.

The currency reflects a much deeper matter, though, and that is the matter of ownership. It involves the matter of governance. It includes the matter of ultimate allegiance by the citizens and rule by the authorities. While the cows, sheep, and the pastures may not differ from one side of the border to the other, the governments of these nations differ significantly. Where authority lies and how that authority can be applied matters.

Visiting Ireland brought this insight to my mind. While a battle for authority can often pop up between nations, states, or regions in our world, a larger conflict looms higher up. That is the conflict in the spiritual realm itself. It is a conflict for spiritual authority and the right to rule. A battle is being waged between God and the enemy, Satan. As believers we know God has ultimate authority, but that doesn't stop Satan from waging war. We see this war playing out in the Scriptures and in our lives.

To review, kingdom authority is *the divinely delegated right and responsibility for believers to act on God's behalf in ruling His creation underneath the Lordship of Jesus Christ.* What changes when we begin to take hold of our kingdom authority?

Have you ever embraced your kingdom authority? If so, how has that benefited your spiritual life? If not, why not?

Name some strategies Satan uses to limit or reduce the use of spiritual authority in believers.

Let's turn our attention to a biblical example that demonstrates the kind of spiritual battle that's always being waged in the spiritual realm. Did you know that Satan can interfere with our prayer life?

Read Daniel 10:10-14 and answer the following questions:

Then behold, a hand touched me and shook me on my hands and knees. And he said to me, "Daniel, you who are treasured, understand the words that I am about to tell you and stand at your place, for I have now been sent to you." And when he had spoken this word to me, I stood up trembling. Then he said to me, "Do not be afraid, Daniel, for from the first day that you set your heart on understanding this and on humbling yourself before your God, your words were heard, and I have come in response to your words. But the prince of the kingdom of Persia was withstanding me for twenty-one days; then behold, Michael, one of the chief princes, came to help me, for I had been left there with the kings of Persia. Now I have come to explain to you what will happen to your people in the latter days, for the vision pertains to the days still future."
DANIEL 10:10-14

In this passage, we enter into the middle of Daniel's prayer life. He was in his eighties and God gave him a glimpse of a future conflict. The "prince of the kingdom of Persia" was not a human ruler in Persia, but a demonic spirit seeking to influence the political affairs of the earth. The battle was real but God had the upper hand.

How did Satan interfere with Daniel receiving the answer
to his prayer? How long did this interference last?

Does this length of time surprise or concern you in any way? How might
this relate to the prayers we offer that haven't been answered?

Unless you and I are aware that Satan actively schemes to disarm us of spiritual authority, we might naively assume that our prayers are just hitting the ceiling because God doesn't care. God does care. God heard and answered Daniel's prayers. But the answer to those prayers wasn't immediate, it was delayed for several weeks. But delayed doesn't always mean denied.

What comfort did God's angel Michael provide Daniel in this
passage? What comfort should that provide for us?

Notice the touch and comfort from God in this passage. Daniel was reassured and affirmed in his struggle. Daniel was called "you who are treasured." This passage illustrates that though our prayers may be momentarily thwarted, our kingdom authority is never threatened. If all Daniel saw was the delay, he would have missed God's dedication and deliverance. Spiritual warfare takes place continually. To the degree that you understand how that conflict works itself out you will also know how to effectively navigate it. Satan loves to try and trick followers of Christ out of accessing their full spiritual authority. Satan seeks to interrupt our spiritual lives in a number of ways beyond our prayer lives.

What kind of strategies have you seen or experienced
Satan use to confuse or limit kingdom authority?

What would be a good way to remind yourself or others
that issues you encounter may actually be rooted in
Satan's schemes to disarm you of spiritual authority?

Satan gets us to squander our spiritual authority by leading us to fight the wrong battles. Satan loves to get us caught up in fighting other people such as our family members, spouse, or different demographics or groups of people based on identity politics. But when we fall for his schemes, we wind up fighting the wrong war and the wrong opponent. Understanding who the enemy is helps you to be equipped to defeat the enemy. If we're fighting the wrong battle, we won't win the war.

Closing

As we come to a close on today's personal reflection, take a moment to pray. Spend some time in prayer asking God to align your heart and spirit with Him so that you can access the spiritual authority He has for you. You might also want to pray for the eyes of your heart to be opened to identify the spiritual warfare being waged around you and request discernment on how to respond.

BIBLE STUDY 2

When Normalcy Shouldn't Be the Norm

Have you ever ordered something online only to have it get held up somewhere in the process? You expected to get it the next day, or even in a few days. With the onset of global supply chain issues, our shipping expectations have had to adjust. Things don't arrive as quickly as they used to.

But as time moves on and days turn to weeks, while still the item hasn't arrived, it could cause you to think that something else is going on above and beyond supply chain issues. You probably look at the tracking information to try and locate your item. If nothing shows up, and if enough days have passed, you may stop looking at the tracking information as frequently as you did at first. Especially if the delay lasts several weeks.

I can only imagine what Daniel must have felt when he had prayed to God but did not hear any real response for twenty-one days. That's three full weeks, on a pretty significant prayer need. Did Daniel feel abandoned? Did he feel forgotten? Did he think there might be a glitch in the system? I'm curious if Daniel even began to doubt God's interest in him. Or His willingness to help out.

The good thing about Scripture is that we don't have to guess. Daniel chapter 10 gives us insight into how Daniel felt during that time of waiting.

Read Daniel 10:2-3 and answer the following questions:

In those days, I, Daniel, had been mourning for three entire weeks. I did not eat any tasty food, nor did meat or wine enter my mouth, nor did I use any ointment at all until the entire three weeks were completed.
DANIEL 10:2-3

What was Daniel's overall demeanor during the
three weeks he waited on God's answer?

Have you ever had to wait on an unanswered prayer, which caused you personal distress? Describe the thoughts you had toward God and toward the situation during that time.

How did Daniel's concern and grief show up in his habits?

Daniel entered a season of mourning to wait on God. The word for *mourning* refers to how one would respond to the death of a family member. Daniel fasted which was normal, but went even further by refusing to clean himself (this is what is meant by ointment). Daniel agonized as he waited.

What does Daniel's grief tell you about the importance of the prayer request?

When have you been in a season like Daniel was in? What changes occurred? How did these changes affect your relationship with God?

When you or I desperately desire an answer to a prayer need, it will often affect what we eat, when we eat, or even how well we sleep. Rather than spend that time worrying, we ought to use these behavioral changes as a reminder to fast and pray. They ought to remind us to go before the Lord more frequently in prayer, asking for His response. What's more, they ought to motivate us to examine our lives and alignment under God. Are we trusting God and embracing His kingdom authority and our ability to wield it? It can be a time for introspection as we seek God and His answer to our prayer need.

> How does prayer and making our requests known to
> God connect us to God and His Kingdom plans?

The delay in God's reply pushed Daniel into a period of mourning and persistent seeking of the Lord. The interesting thing to remember, though, is that God did reply when Daniel prayed initially. It was only that His response got intercepted by demonic forces, causing the agonizing delay Daniel found himself in (see Daniel 10:13). Yet because Daniel responded with intentional pursuit rather than apathetic dismissal of his situation, he willingly tapped into the kingdom authority available to him.

I am sure that you and I have prayer requests hanging out there in the heavenly places that are stuck there not because God has been slow to answer but because His answers are caught up in a spiritual battle being waged in the heavenlies. Yet in the delay we are not disarmed. We can fervently seek God's face like Daniel. Spiritual authority is ours because Jesus won it for us at the cross. Seeking God unites us with God's power.

As we unite with God's power we grow in our faith. Spiritual maturity prepares us to press into God and into His ways in the heat of the battle. It forges our bond with Him and helps us trust Him more. Consider this example from James.

> *A prayer of a righteous person, when it is brought about, can*
> *accomplish much. Elijah was a man with a nature like ours, and*
> *he prayed earnestly that it would not rain, and it did not rain on*
> *the earth for three years and six months. Then he prayed again,*
> *and the sky poured rain and the earth produced its fruit.*
> JAMES 5:16-18

Do you think a person's spiritual maturity and intentions impact the way God supplies answers to prayers? How so?

If you want to reclaim what the enemy has stolen from you or holds hostage from you, pursue God as a kingdom disciple—a verbal, visible follower of Jesus Christ. Kingdom disciples embrace kingdom authority and pursue God in grief or in great triumph because they trust the ruler of the kingdom and His goals.

When have circumstances in your life led you to lock onto God and press into Him? What did you learn about Him and His rule in that time?

Obedience to God and alignment underneath His kingdom rule opens the doors in the heavenly realm that can't be opened without God's help. It frees up angelic help to come to our aid, oftentimes with answers to our prayers. That's what spiritual, kingdom authority entails. It entails the wisdom and discernment needed to tap into God's authority and embrace His rule.

Closing

Pray right now and ask God to reveal to you what areas of your life could use some spiritual growth and development so that you are in alignment under Him. Also ask God for a greater fervency when it comes to continuing to seek Him for the answers to your prayers that have gone unanswered. Praise Him for the times He has shown up in your life in amazing ways.

WEEK 2

THE OPPONENT TO KINGDOM AUTHORITY

Start

Welcome to group session 2.

When have you had to face an opponent in a game or a competition?

How would your game be negatively impacted
if you didn't understand the rules?

If you have watched professional wrestling for any length of time, you should know by now that the outcome has been determined before the match begins. (Sorry if this is your first time hearing this.) Part of the fun of watching these matches is the match itself, not as much as the outcome, because the wrestlers are free to go at it in the confines of the victory already designed. Knowing the rules doesn't help you win. But it would be a lot different if the wrestlers ever forgot who was the predetermined winner!

If you have studied Scripture or read your Bible in any depth at all, you also know by now that the outcome in spiritual warfare has been determined. Jesus Christ has secured the victory through His death on the cross and resurrection. When we go up against Satan or his demons in spiritual warfare, we are not fighting for victory. We are fighting from a position of victory. Our victory is secured in Jesus Christ.

The problems occur when we forget that and start fighting in our own strength rather than in the victorious authority found in Christ. We're victorious only when we know how and through whom our victory lies.

How can understanding the strategy or rules
of the game help you secure a victory?

Ask someone to pray then watch group session 2.

Watch

Follow along as you watch video session 2.

Discuss

Use the following questions to discuss the video teaching.

One of the issues we have exercising our God-given kingdom authority is that there is an opponent to our kingdom authority—the devil. The Bible describes him as a thief who came to steal, kill, and destroy (John 10:10) and a lion looking for prey (1 Peter 5:8).

How should knowing the devil's tactics prepare us to face his attacks?

Though it is easy and even natural to focus on the devil when we are being spiritually attacked, why should we focus on Jesus instead?

Jesus knows the outcome in all of the spiritual battles we face. He knows how far He will allow the devil and the devil's demons to go on their leash. But He also knows how far He won't let them go because the outcome and victory has been secured by Him.

It may look scary to us when we are in the middle of spiritual battles, but knowing who holds the leash and who has won the victory ought to give us calm when we instead want to be yelling and screaming because of the chaos around us.

Why do you think it's easy to forget that Jesus is ultimately in control of the spiritual battles and issues we find ourselves in?

How might we act differently during times of chaos caused by the enemy if we trusted that victory is already secured for us by Christ?

The book of Revelation tells us that we have overcome the devil through three God-given means:

And they overcame [the devil] because of the blood of the Lamb and because of the word of their testimony, and they did not love their life even when faced with death.
REVELATION 12:11

What are the three components of spiritual victory Dr. Evans identified in this verse? How would you define each of these?

In the video Dr. Evans explains the three components to living in victory. First, the blood of the Lamb identifies us with Jesus and His sacrifice on the cross which makes us new and seals our identity with Him. Then it goes to the word of our testimony. This means that we hold fast to our commitment to Him. Lastly, it says we overcome Him by not loving our lives even in the face of death. We need to be willing to yield to Christ even if it costs us dearly.

How does knowing Jesus has already overcome the devil and his schemes change our approach to spiritual warfare?

How would reciting the testimony of Christ through meditating and memorizing Scripture strengthen you to face and overcome spiritual opponents?

Share a time when you've held close to Christ in the middle of your spiritual battles.

We'll dive deeper into these truths in our personal study, but for now, let's end our time together in prayer.

Prayer

Lord Jesus, You are the declared winner. We aren't fighting the issues in our lives from a place of spiritual defeat. When we're aligned under You, we're fighting from a place of spiritual victory. Help us to understand and access the assurance and power that come from our identification with You, Jesus. In Your name, amen.

HIT THE STREETS

The Right Key

If you have ever tried to open up a door with the wrong key, you know the frustration that comes from thinking you are doing something right but not getting the results you expected. Sometimes a person can even jam a door by trying to use the wrong key for too long. As they push it in too far and try to muscle it to turn, it could actually break the key itself.

Sometimes we try to access the kingdom authority that is ours with the wrong key. We try our own wit, worldly wisdom, or sheer effort to defeat the enemy. But the wrong key will never win at spiritual war. The only way we can obtain the victory that has already been gained on our behalf is by using the key of Jesus Christ.

God has given us three things we can do to tap into Christ's victory on the cross. He has laid them out for us clearly in Revelation 12:10-11. Here are three ways you can apply these truths in your own life:

1. Invite the power of the blood of Jesus into your situation. You can do this through regularly abiding in Jesus and actively trusting Him and by participating in corporate worship and communion.

   How often do you invite the blood of Jesus into your situation?

   What situation do you need to invite Him into right now?

2. Speak to others whenever you can concerning the testimony that Jesus has over and in your own life. Make His name known through your conversations, what you post online, and even in what you tell yourself.

   Who do you need to tell about what Jesus is doing in your life?
   (Hint: it might be a friend that's facing a spiritual battle.)

3. Relinquish your need to always place your wants and desires over God's will for your life, even at the expense of your wants and desires. In doing so, you yield yourself to God and do not count your life as more important than the advancement of His kingdom agenda and the magnification of His glory.

What are some areas where you're placing your desires
for your life over God's desires for your life?

If you will commit to do these three things regularly and with a sincere heart, you will find that Jesus is vital and near to you in the challenges and trials you face. It is in Christ that you tap into the kingdom authority to overcome the opponent who seeks to prevent you from living out the fullness of your Christian life.

The Accuser and Deceiver

You and I are living in a day of mass deception. People are being tricked about their gender and identity. They are being deceived about the definition of a family and marriage. People are being hoodwinked on how to handle their finances. The world is facing an onslaught of deception. Many are buying it hook, line, and sinker and then trying to hook others into the same deception. We are being duped by the devil, even as we claim to know "my truth." In fact, people will defend "their truth" to the death these days. Unfortunately, it is often to their own death—whether that's the a death of emotional well-being, health, financial stability, relational harmony, or even physical death.

Satan is good at this game. He manipulates and twists our thoughts to advance his evil agenda. Satan feeds off of the devastation and destruction he creates. He doesn't want to just bully us. Rather, he seeks to defeat us. He wants a claim to his victories over God's followers. He wants to devour us.

Read 1 Peter 5:8 and answer the following questions:

Be of sober spirit, be on the alert. Your adversary, the devil, prowls around like a roaring lion, seeking someone to devour.
1 PETER 5:8

The term *adversary* is a word that would've been used
to describe an opponent in a lawsuit. What does this
teach us about who Satan is and what he is like?

What are some strategies Satan uses to devour those he targets?

34

Based on what you just identified, list four ways you can be of "sober spirit" or "on the alert" to Satan's schemes in your daily life.

How does believing Satan's deception cause us to be ineffective disciples of Jesus?

A spiritual battle goes on all around us. In it, Satan seeks to prevent God's followers—to prevent *you*—from experiencing what He provided for you on the cross—the kingdom authority that comes from placing your faith in Jesus. Satan seeks to do this through deception and clever but untrue arguments. He's a liar. We've knows this since the garden of Eden. He loves to twist Gods words and manipulate our thoughts. He is both an accuser and a deceiver.

Satan desires to deceive the whole world. None of us are exempt. If you are here reading this page and participating in this Bible study—then you are a target of the opposition, the devil. Unfortunately, his schemes are as clever as they are numerous.

Why does Satan rely on deception to get believers off track from living out their kingdom purpose?

Share about a time you were deceived by the devil only to discover it after the fact. What did you learn in that experience?

Is there something you struggle with in your thoughts, emotions,
or relationships right now where it's possible that you have
been deceived? What Scripture could speak to this situation?

Before we go much further on such a sensitive subject, I want to clarify something. I am not saying that every deception, disappointment, difficulty, or death is outside of God's will and caused by Satan. Sometimes these are caused by our own sin and willful disobedience, other times God sovereignly allows challenges and losses in our lives for His purposes, as He works them out for good, causing us to be conformed to the image of Christ (see Romans 8:28-29).

However, it's true that some sicknesses, disappointments, difficulties, and even death do take place because of spiritual warfare, where Satan or his demons seek to block a believer from seeking God's purposes or stifle their ability to see God's work. While that is a discouraging and troubling truth to realize, there is also good news. The good news is that you have access to the kingdom authority you need in order to silence the accuser and fight back against his schemes. To whatever degree that Satan is bringing havoc into your life, God has endowed you with supernatural power and guidance to keep Satan from obscuring God's will, purposes, and plan. This mechanism is what we know as kingdom authority.

What are some ways to discern the root of an issue you are facing
so you can better understand how to address it spiritually?

What happens when you choose to ignore the
spiritual root of issues and conflict in your life?

In your own words, what does it mean to "access kingdom authority"?

On a scale of 1-10 (with 10 being the most) where are you in living a life that accesses kingdom authority?

1   10

What are some things you may need to adjust to move closer to a 10?

Closing

As we close this session, spend some time praying about how you can more fully identify with Jesus Christ and access the spiritual authority He has given you through His life, death, and resurrection. Access your beliefs and thought patterns and measure them against the truth of God's Word. Have you been deceived in any way? If the answer is yes, spend time in prayer repenting and asking God to give you clarity on His will for your life—including your thoughts, words, and actions.

BIBLE STUDY 2

Three Ways to Overcome

The book of Revelation provides us with some of the greatest insights into the battles that take place for spiritual authority. It goes into many of the details involved in the clash of kingdoms taking place all around us. The book of Revelation is a statement book, not only about this war in the heavenly realm, but about God's ultimate kingdom authority. We can see throughout its pages that Satan will be removed and defeated once and for all. But what we also see is that right now, Satan roams free. Before we turn our attention to Revelation, let's look together in the book of Job to gain some insight about how Satan operates.

Read Job 1:6-8 and answer the following questions:

Now there was a day when the sons of God came to present themselves before the LORD, and Satan also came among them. The LORD said to Satan, "From where do you come?" Then Satan answered the LORD and said, "From roaming about on the earth and walking around on it."
JOB 1:6-8

What do these verses teach us about Satan?

Though it may seem odd to spend so much time considering
the opponent to kingdom authority, why is it helpful
to recognize what Satan can and cannot do?

The "sons of God" are a council of heavenly beings that present themselves to God like a king's attendants would meet with him. Notice that the Bible says, "Satan also came among them" (v.6). Though under God's ultimate sovereign control, Satan has some ability to travel freely on a spiritual plane in addition to his ability to impact events on earth.

Revelation chapter 12 provides further description and strategy to combat Satan and his ploys. This unique, and often overlooked, chapter gives us a glimpse into the cosmic clash which our eyes cannot see and our ears do not hear, even though it is raging all around us. Reading Revelation gives us a peek into that which is beyond our natural ability to recognize or see physically. It also helps us to more fully understand our role in this unseen drama playing out so that we will be able to wield the power and authority given to us in the name of Jesus.

Read Revelation 12:9-12 and answer the following questions:

And the great dragon was thrown down, the serpent of old who is called the devil and Satan, who deceives the whole world; he was thrown down to the earth, and his angels were thrown down with him. Then I heard a loud voice in heaven, saying, "Now the salvation, and the power, and the kingdom of our God and the authority of His Christ have come, for the accuser of our brothers and sisters has been thrown down, he who accuses them before our God day and night. And they overcame him because of the blood of the Lamb and because of the word of their testimony, and they did not love their life even when faced with death. For this reason, rejoice, O heavens and you who dwell in them. Woe to the earth and the sea, because the devil has come down to you with great wrath, knowing that he has only a short time."
REVELATION 12:9-12

What do the words "the kingdom of our God and the authority of His Christ" teach us about kingdom authority?

What do these verses reveal about the limits of Satan's authority?

In the group study, we identified three strategies God has given us to overcome the devil and his works. Beyond knowing the devil and his schemes we need to recognize and memorize the mechanisms God has given us to exercise our kingdom authority.

Review and reword each of the following strategies we find in Revelation 12 in your own words, being mindful to apply it to everyday life: they overcame him because of . . .

the blood of the Lamb . . .

the word of their testimony . . .

and because they did not love their life even when faced with death.

A lot of people are content to relate to Jesus as a kind of figurehead or mascot rather than as Lord and Savior. To be connected with Jesus we need to be anchored in His blood, our testimony, and a total surrender to His will. God doesn't need more fans. He is looking for serious kingdom followers. Jesus doesn't desire convenient Christians. He wants committed Christians willing to be linked up with Him. Authority comes through surrender.

Read Jesus's words then answer the following questions:

Then Jesus said to His disciples, "If anyone wishes to come after Me, he must deny himself, take up his cross, and follow Me."
MATTHEW 16:24

What does obedience to Jesus's words in Matthew 16:24 look like practically?

How are you applying this verse to your life?

If you want to unleash God's kingdom authority in your life, if you want to overcome Satan's accusations as he stands at the door of your purpose and prospects—you need to live covered under the blood of Jesus, while testifying to the work of Jesus and submitting your life's desires to Christ. When you do that, you will reclaim what the enemy has stolen and then some. You will step into the pathways of a new opportunity as you witness the power from on high dispel and overturn the opposition in your way as you head to a greater kingdom purpose.

What is your "kingdom purpose"? What has God called
you to do, as best you understand it right now?

Are you embracing your kingdom purpose? If not, what
do you need to do differently to start living it out?

Let me tell you an easy way to start living out your kingdom purpose. Draw close to Jesus Christ. As you get closer to Him and abide in Him, you will discover that your purpose draws close to you. Rather than seeking your purpose under a rock or through books or a fervent pursuit, just draw near to the One who holds it in His hand. That way, you will also be close to the One who has the power to defeat the enemy because His is the authority of the kingdom.

Closing

As we close out this week's session, spend some time praying for clarity of purpose and focus in your life. Ask God to cover you with the power, protection, and authority of the blood of Jesus. That's a prayer you can pray regularly. Seek to be more intentional about sharing the word of your testimony with others, and if that makes you nervous in any way, ask God to give you strength as well as opportunities to do so.

WEEK 3

THE BASIS OF KINGDOM AUTHORITY

Start

Welcome to group session 3.

The seventeenth century saw a litany of battles, wars, rebellions, and uprisings as nations fought for power and control. One of these long-fought battles took place at Ross Castle, where this session was filmed. England sought to take over the land the Irish claimed for themselves. At the lead of many of these battles was a man known as Lieutenant General Oliver Cromwell.

Legend had it that the castle would one day be defeated by an army which reached it by boat. Knowing this legend, Cromwell played to the psyche of his opponents and sought to overpower them where they were the weakest. They had arms. They had defenses. They had security. But they lacked truth. They lacked a belief in their ability to withstand. When Cromwell's army approached them by boat, the remaining soldiers and leaders at Ross Castle surrendered because their defeat had already been secured in their mind.

> When have you made a decision based on false
> information? What was the result?

> What are some core truths that guide how you
> respond to hardship and conflict?

The Irish had all they needed for victory, their castle was secure and well defended, but they were defeated because they defaulted to false belief. As Christ followers we have the authority. It has been secured for us on a stronger foundation than any castle or fortress—the cross of Jesus Christ. Understanding our victory is crucial to exercising our authority.

> Ask someone to pray then watch group session 3.

Watch

Take notes as you watch video session 3.

Discuss

Use the following questions to discuss the video teaching.

The castle where this session was filmed is called Ross Castle. It was the last holdout of the Irish against the English invasion of the seventeeth century. The Irish lost as their last stronghold fell. However, there was another time when the last stronghold was defeated and the authority of heaven was demonstrated on earth.

Read Colossians 2:13-15 together.

> *[Jesus] made you alive together with Him, having forgiven us all our wrongdoings, having canceled the certificate of debt consisting of decrees against us, which was hostile to us; and He has taken it out of the way, having nailed it to the cross. When He had disarmed the rulers and authorities, He made a public display of them, having triumphed over them through Him.*
> COLOSSIANS 2:13-15

List all that Jesus accomplished at Calvary based on this passage.

What does it look like to actively embrace the victory that Jesus won that day?

The cross of Jesus Christ represents the final blow to hell, when heaven made its ultimate move to bring the victory of God for the benefit, salvation, and deliverance of humanity. The cross represents the greatest transfer of authority in all of history. Through the cross Jesus secured an eternal victory and now He grants His followers His authority to live for Him and His kingdom agenda.

If Jesus has secured authority for us, what are some reasons that we don't exercise that authority?

Why do so many of us live as if the "rulers and authorities"— Satan and his forces—still have power over us?

Jesus's victory is our victory. We just need to walk in it. In the video, Dr. Evans spoke about how Ross Castle had the look of authority, but didn't have actual authority. Many believers operate in the same way. We are content to have the appearance of authority with none of the power.

> Why do we settle for the appearance of kingdom authority
> instead of the power of kingdom authority?

Jesus has the divine right of a king. While castles of men come one day and are gone the next, they may still stand but the power that they used to exemplify is no longer manifesting itself. There's another authority manifested now and that is the ascension of Jesus Christ. He is busy ruling from heaven with His authority to benefit His people on earth. Jesus's ascension means that He is still calling the shots.

> What impact should Jesus's reign in heaven have on our lives on earth?

> What are you afraid of or troubled by that could be
> resolved if you simply trusted that there is a King in
> heaven who has provided for your every need?

Let's start out our study this week in prayer.

Prayer

Lord, we praise You for the victory You secured on the cross. We praise You that You have made this truth real and available to anyone who desires to know it. Let us walk boldly in the confidence that we are citizens in a victorious heavenly kingdom because we serve the King of kings and Lord of lords. In Jesus's name, amen.

HIT THE STREETS

Embracing Kingdom Authority

On the cross Jesus did everything necessary to secure and fill His followers with kingdom authority. To regularly access this authority and live with its benefits we need to abide in Christ. Staying close to God's Word can help you continually access the kingdom authority Christ secured.

1. Identify the people in your life who know the truth and who can help give you wisdom and discernment concerning issues or decisions in your life. Take time to talk with them and be open to their advice and influence. Ask them for help and wisdom on how to view things from a spiritual perspective.

2. Ask God to reveal wisdom to you through His Word as you seek Him on a regular basis. Becoming wise entails intaking wisdom so that when the rubber meets the road you can pull on your stored resources.

3. Make a list of things which help you to stay close to God's Word and enjoy the habit of daily time in Scripture. Write down the truths that God teaches you as you study His Word then revisit what you write down, especially in times of confusion or weakness.

If you will commit to doing these three things on a regular basis, you will begin to see the power of kingdom authority made manifest in your life. This power is rooted in Christ's victory on the cross. You access this victory through a close, intimate, and abiding relationship with both the living Word and the written Word. In doing so, you tap into the wisdom and discernment needed to overcome Satan's schemes and tactics which seek to entrap you in deception, distraction, or distortion.

The evil kingdoms of this world may look like they are in charge. But Jesus stripped them of authority at the cross. Now, all the evil one can do is lure you through looks or defeat you through deception. Satan maintains the look of authority only, not actual authority. The actual kingdom authority is in the hands of Jesus Christ. Through the death and resurrection of Jesus Christ, hell—who thought it would have a victory and who thought its kingdom would come out as a winner—found out it was aced by grace. It was defeated by the Son of the living God.

What steps will you take over the next week
to bring God's Word into your life?

If you are already seeking God daily through His
Word, how are you seeking to apply it?

What promises from Scripture are you trusting to connect you
to Christ and apply His saving work to your daily life?

BIBLE STUDY 1

An Awesome Saturday

Though Christ has won the ultimate victory—the basis of our kingdom authority, many of us still live as though we are under the curse of the first man: Adam. The "first Adam" fumbled, bringing sin, death, and destruction to the human race. But at the cross, on a weekend never to be forgotten, Jesus Christ changed the trajectory of history. Jesus as the "second Adam" reversed the curse brought on by the first (1 Corinthians 15:20-28).

This transfer of kingdom authority is recorded for us in the book of Colossians, where we uncover more on the relevancy of what the cross is and why it matters so much as the basis of kingdom authority. Through the cross, kingdom authority has been transferred from God to His people because of the work of Jesus.

Read Colossians 2:8-15 and answer the following questions:

See to it that no one takes you captive through philosophy and empty deception in accordance with human tradition, in accordance with the elementary principles of the world, rather than in accordance with Christ. For in Him all the fullness of Deity dwells in bodily form, and in Him you have been made complete, and He is the head over every ruler and authority; and in Him you were also circumcised with a circumcision performed without hands, in the removal of the body of the flesh by the circumcision of Christ, having been buried with Him in baptism, in which you were also raised up with Him through faith in the working of God, who raised Him from the dead. And when you were dead in your wrongdoings and the uncircumcision of your flesh, He made you alive together with Him, having forgiven us all our wrongdoings, having canceled out the certificate of debt consisting of decrees against us, which was hostile to us; and He has taken it out of the way, having nailed it to the cross. When He had disarmed the rulers and authorities, He made a public display of them, having triumphed over them through Him.
COLOSSIANS 2:8-15

What are some common ways that you can be held "captive through philosophy and empty deception"?

What does it mean that "all the fullness of deity" dwells in Jesus and that He is "the head over all rule and authority"?

How does it make you feel to know that your Savior holds the ultimate authority over all things?

Has there been a time in your life where you have tapped into Christ's kingdom authority and seen it overrule your emotions, situations, relationships, or anything else? What did you learn from that experience?

We all know about Sunday morning and the resurrection of Jesus Christ. His resurrection gave us the receipt of our victory over sin and death. Sunday morning was where it became both vindicated and validated that the payment on Friday of Christ's death on the cross was accepted by God Almighty. But between Good Friday and Resurrection Sunday sits Awesome Saturday.

We don't hear a lot about Awesome Saturday but it is a key aspect to the subject of authority. In fact, 1 Peter 3:19 says that when Jesus died on the cross and prior to His resurrection, He went to hell and proclaimed victory to the captive souls in prison. Thus, after Jesus had died on Friday, and while waiting for His body to get up out of the grave on Sunday, His Spirit declared victory on Saturday! Hell was informed: you lose and heaven wins.

Jesus declared the ultimate defeat of Satan and Satan's authority. Because when Adam sinned, he abdicated the authority of the rule of earth over to the devil. In the present age, the Bible refers to Satan as the god of this world, the prince of the power of the air (Ephesians 2:2). In this role, he seeks to lead the world into chaos, sin, and despair.

But Jesus demonstrated His full and final authority over death and hell on the cross. He has all authority, and He gives His followers the authority He has.

Read Matthew 28:18 and answer the following questions:

And Jesus came up and spoke to them, saying, "All authority in heaven and on earth has been given to Me."
MATTHEW 28:18

What are some ways Jesus's ultimate authority shows up in spiritual battles that take place in our culture?

Describe a situation where you have witnessed Jesus's authority overrule the enemy's attack either in your own life, or someone else's, or in the Bible? What can you learn from that?

Since Jesus has authority over all in both heaven and earth, He is the One calling the shots. He's not only calling the shots in the sweet by-and-by. But He's also now calling the shots on earth. Jesus is calling the shots in both heaven and in history. He's calling the shots in eternity and in time.

You know what that means for you personally? It means that Jesus Christ has the last say in your personal trials and tribulations. It means that He is the final Ruler. He can overrule anything that hell wants to bring your way in your life, emotions, relationships, and circumstances. It means that you, as a follower of Jesus Christ, have the opportunity and the responsibility to see what His kingdom authority looks like on full display.

Read 1 John 4:4.

You are from God, little children, and have overcome them; because greater is He who is in you than he who is in the world.
1 JOHN 4:4

How tapped in to Jesus are you so that His authority
in you can overcome the opposition you face?

_____

1 (least)   10 (most)

Read 1 John 5:4.

For whoever has been born of God overcomes the world; and this is the victory that has overcome the world: our faith.
1 JOHN 5:4

What is your level of faith in Jesus Christ and His
ultimate victory and authority over Satan?

_____

1 (least)   10 (most)

Closing

Close out today's session by being honest in your level of faith in Jesus. Where you have unbelief or doubt in His ultimate kingdom authority, ask God to increase your faith. Let Him know you give Him the opportunity to place things in your life which will help to develop your trust in Him as the ultimate kingdom authority over everything. Then, buckle up as He teaches You that His power and authority can overcome anything Satan seeks to put in your way on your path toward increased spiritual maturity.

BIBLE STUDY 2

Jesus, the Interceder

Far too often in spiritual warfare, we want to nurse our wounds rather than rebuild after a spiritual loss. We want to blame others because we think we are fighting people, systems, or even our own emotions. But in reality, God has allowed the devil to have his way with us in order to provide an opportunity for us to realign with God. Because of our innate connection with sinfulness and pride, God often accomplishes His purposes through our pain.

Often, our sin and disobedience puts us in a place where we are ripe to be sifted by Satan (Luke 22:31). God can use your struggles to show you who you really are. He can allow Satan to break you down so that you can experience the growth that comes from surrender.

The book of Hebrews tells us that suffering can be a kind of discipline from God because we are His children. If you're a parent or have been around young children, you know their mistakes and missteps provide them an opportunity to grow and change course. The choice is up to you in how you respond after a spiritual implosion in your life. You can sit, sulk, and sour. Or you can get up and grow up, spiritually.

What we can learn in times of spiritual defeat when we have been duped by the devil is that we must depend on Jesus for our full victory. We access kingdom authority through Christ.

Read John 15:5 and answer the following questions:

"I am the vine, you are the branches; the one who remains in Me, and I in him bears much fruit, for apart from Me you can do nothing."
JOHN 15:5

How can experiencing spiritual defeat produce greater
reliance on Jesus with regard to kingdom authority?

What does it look like on a practical level in your life to abide in Jesus?

Spiritual brokenness often puts us into a position to find the true spiritual power Jesus offers through kingdom authority, because brokenness leads us to understand that God is God, and we aren't. This is an important lesson for each of us. It's a hard lesson but it is critical in fully living for Jesus. It's critical for accessing and employing kingdom authority.

Why is it important to turn to Jesus for kingdom
authority in the midst of spiritual warfare?

Read the following verses and write them in your own words, taking
time to explain how they relate to our exercising kingdom authority.

For our struggle is not against flesh and blood, but against the
rulers, against the powers, against the world forces of this darkness,
against the spiritual forces of wickedness in the heavenly places.
EPHESIANS 6:12

Summary:

For the weapons of our warfare are not of the flesh, but
divinely powerful for the destruction of fortresses.
2 CORINTHIANS 10:4

Summary:

"Behold, I have given you authority to walk on snakes and scorpions, and
authority over all the power of the enemy, and nothing will injure you."
LUKE 10:19

Summary:

I've got good news for you if you feel like you've blown it and don't know how to get back what the enemy has stolen, either through your own spiritual immaturity or sin. God will meet you where you are. He will meet you there as long as you are honest with Him and look to Him to access the kingdom authority you need.

When you look to Jesus Christ, He can give you back the years the locusts have stolen (Joel 2:25-26). He knows how to turn things, tweak things, remake things, and restore things. You can get back your dignity. You can get back your energy. You can get back your calling. You can get it all back because Jesus knows how to do just that. And He always lives to intercede on your behalf.

According to Hebrews 7:25,

Therefore He is able also to save forever those who come to God
through Him, since He always lives to make intercession for them.
HEBREWS 7:25

Describe what it means for Jesus to intercede
on your behalf before the Lord.

How often do you rely on Jesus's intercessory prayer and power? What would change if you relied on Him more often?

We can take comfort in the truth that Jesus lives to help you and me—to intercede on our behalf. In fact, He calls this high calling His Priestly duty. The job of the priest in the Old Testament was to serve as a mediator between a sinful people and a holy God. The way He served as a mediator between sinful people and a holy God was through the sacrificial system.

The priest would offer up an animal on a specified day such as the Day of Atonement so that God's judgment against sin would be diverted due to this sacrifice. God's wrath would then be held back so that He could show favor to His people because an acceptable sacrifice had been made.

The sacrificial system was a good system but it was also a temporary system. It was sign along the road to point to what Jesus accomplished on the cross. There Jesus said "it is finished" (John 19:30). The work of redemption is done. In other words, no more sacrifices are needed. Jesus can now "always live" to be the Intercessor on behalf of sinful Christians before a holy God. Because of His intercession, He has diverted God's wrath from reaching us in order that we might experience God's favor and access His kingdom authority.

Closing

Let's close out our time together in prayer, asking for Christ's interceding power to make itself known more fully in your life. Spend a moment drawing near to Jesus and thanking Him for His work on the cross and His resurrection. Ask Him to reveal the power of His resurrection to you on a more regular basis so you can come to identify His presence and authority more in your everyday circumstances. In this way, you will rely on Him and His kingdom authority in a more authentic and consistent way.

THE KEY TO KINGDOM AUTHORITY

Start

Welcome to group session 4.

Describe your understanding of what it means to surrender to God.

Cobb, Ireland was the last port of call for the *Titanic*. When the ship sunk over fifteen hundred people lost their lives, seventy-nine of whom had boarded the ship in Cobb, Ireland. As you're about to hear in the video teaching session, part of the tragedy of the *Titanic* involved a missing key to the ship's crows nest which stored the ship's binoculars, which would've allowed the crew to see the iceberg in the distance.

The *Titanic* disaster was tied to a missing key. The failure to engage kingdom authority is also related to a missing key. Everybody wants the authority, sure. But far too often they want it without the key. The key is surrender—yielding all of life to the lordship of Jesus Christ. Without surrender, there is no authority.

What are some common hindrances to living
with complete surrender to God?

Ask someone to pray then watch group session 4.

Watch

Take notes as you watch video session 4.

Discuss

Use the following questions to discuss the video teaching.

Many Christians have not used the key of surrender to access the kingdom authority God has for them. As a result, they fail to fully experience the benefits of Christ's lordship.

Why is Jesus concerned with our spiritual surrender?

What does it mean for Jesus Christ to be "Lord"?

Describe a person who is fully surrendered to Jesus Christ.

Dr. Evans defined surrender as *yielding all of life to the lordship of Jesus Christ*. Without understanding and embracing spiritual surrender you will miss out on the joy and blessing of being a kingdom disciple. If you've ever spent time with someone who is fully surrendered to Christ, you know that Jesus is able to do exceedingly more with surrender than restraint. Being surrendered helps us see where God is at work and allows us to be a conduit for that work as we exercise the power that comes from surrender.

Can you share a Bible verse that helps you when
you are struggling to fully surrender?

What keeps some Christians from giving all of themselves to Jesus?

If you are acting like a part-time Christian and not a full-time saint, then your access to experience Christ's authority, rule, and governance will be diminished at best. Many Christians wonder why some Christians seem to get more prayers answered, seem to have more direction, to have more clarity, to operate with more confidence, and to be more in tune with God and His work. The key is surrender. Notice Jesus's words:

Then Jesus said to His disciples, "If anyone wants to come after Me, he must deny himself, take up his cross, and follow Me. For whoever wants to save his life will lose it; but whoever loses his life for My sake will find it."
MATTHEW 16:24-25

This passage is well-known, but less embraced and obeyed.
Why do we find Jesus's call to discipleship challenging?

If the key is surrender, why do we tend to imagine
the key is something much more complicated?

Unfortunately, many Christians have not fully surrendered to the lordship of Jesus Christ. Lack of surrender directly leads to their lack of kingdom authority. For the Christian, surrender is obedience to the call of Christ. Jesus's words to us in Matthew are for all Christians at all times. To embrace Jesus is to embrace His lordship and our surrender. Until we surrender, we will be missing the best of what God has for us.

What are some discipleship practices and spiritual habits
that lead us to be more willing to live fully surrendered?

Let's close our group session in prayer.

Prayer

Lord, help us to truly know how our surrender to the lordship of Jesus Christ allows us to experience the grace and power of kingdom authority. Lead us to be affective kingdom disciples who faithfully execute the authority that You have vested in us. Give us the courage to surrender to Jesus in all areas of our lives. In Jesus's name, amen.

HIT THE STREETS
Lost the Key

The illusion of control is one of the greatest self-deceptions. We feel that we can bootstrap our way through life and make decisions without God's direction or guidance. We want to rely on our own thoughts, wisdom, and motivations to show us what to do. But when we do, we willingly relinquish our right to surrender. We miss out on the blessing of kingdom authority because we've lost the key.

This is why it is so important to keep our hearts focused on Jesus and connected to Him. It is only through spiritual surrender to His lordship that you will discover how great it is to live as a saint who fully utilizes kingdom authority. Take a look at these three tips on how to live a life of surrender to Jesus Christ. Start to implement these in your everyday choices and watch God unleash His power and authority in and through you.

1. Spend regular time in God's Word. You can't surrender to someone if you don't know them and what their values are. Spending time in God's Word enables you to get to know the voice and the values of the Living Word, Jesus Christ.

   What is one truth you've learned recently from God's Word? How is it helping you love and serve Jesus?

2. Speak with Christ. Yes, talk to Him. You don't have to have a time of dedicated, formal prayer to talk with Jesus. His Spirit is with you at all times. Just talk. Tell Him what you are thinking and the things you are wrestling with. Ask Him to show you what He wants you to do or spend your time on. Ask for His guidance. Ask for His tips. Ask Him to show you what it means to live a life of surrender.

   When are the built-in moments of free time you have each day?

What would change about those times if you spoke
to God instead of scrolling on a phone?

3. Listen for His response and look for His presence in your life. Talking with Jesus is a two-way conversation. Just because you cannot see Him physically doesn't mean He has nothing to say. Your spirit will recognize His Spirit when He speaks to you. But you need to give the space and time and focus for your spirit to connect and listen. It is only through listening to Jesus that you can learn from Jesus and surrender your thoughts, words, and actions to Him.

When are the built in times you can pause to listen to Jesus?

Surrender is never easy. We all have our own thoughts and desires which get in the way of a decision to surrender to Jesus. But you can make the process easier by putting into practice these three key things. Spend time in God's Word. Speak with Christ. Listen to Christ. When you do these three things on a regular basis, you will see Him like you've never seen Him before. As a result, surrendering to Him will become easier than it's ever been before as well.

BIBLE STUDY 1

The Ruler over All

One of the main reasons we fail to realize our kingdom authority is because we fail to turn the key. Surrender unlocks the power of Jesus in your life. You need Jesus's power because He is the One who rules over all.

Read Ephesians 1:22-23 and answer the following questions:

And He put all things in subjection under His feet, and made Him head over all things to the church, which is His body, the fullness of Him who fills all in all.
EPHESIANS 1:22-23

What do these verses teach us about Jesus's lordship and control?

All people and all things are subject to Christ. The difference is whether or not we resist. What are some ways we resist His rule?

Embodying kingdom authority entails surrendering to Jesus and recognizing His rightful rule. To be under Christ's feet means we are under His authority, control, and rule. However, just because we are under Christ's rule doesn't mean that we're embracing it or actively participating in it.

Being obedient to Christ's rule and eagerly surrendering to Him puts us in a position to receive from Him and connect His rule to our daily life. Our lives will start to take a different shape because we are more in tune with Him as His desires become our desires and we become the hands and feet for His actions in heaven here on earth.

God only dispenses His kingdom authority from where He sits on high in order to benefit us down here when we live underneath the rule of Jesus Christ. To put it another way, you and I must settle one issue only: the lordship of Jesus Christ, over every area of life. That is the key. Surrendering to the lordship of Jesus is key to everything, spiritually. That is what must be addressed before you unlock and unleash heaven's authority on your behalf.

Heaven's power comes to us when we are operating under Jesus's feet. That means what Jesus says goes. What Jesus wants goes. Jesus's goals are to become your own.

What are some areas of life in which you need to
apply Jesus's authority and dominion?

What might you expect to change if you gave Jesus
more authority and direction over your decisions?

Why would you withhold surrender from Jesus?
How has holding onto control ever benefited you?

One of the issues we face in our culture today is that we have too many AM/FM Christians. They switch frequencies. They are heavenly on Sunday then go secular on Monday. They keep switching frequencies back and forth, and then wonder why they don't get to hear the whole song. The reason they don't experience the blessing that comes from God's kingdom authority is because God won't let anyone two-time Him. He's always Lord, but we're not always willing to be ruled.

If we're in charge then that means we must rely on our own maneuvering and manipulation to make it through life. But if Jesus is Lord (and He is), then we can rely on His power and authority to overrule our impulses and desires that are contrary to His will. Unless Jesus is Lord over our thoughts, words, actions, and decisions, we will treat Him as just another a religious experience to encourage and inspire us, but we will miss out on knowing God truly and intimately.

Read Romans 14:7-9.

For not one of us lives for himself, and not one dies for himself; for if we live, we live for the Lord, or if we die, we die for the Lord; therefore whether we live or die, we are the Lord's. For to this end Christ died and lived again, that He might be Lord both of the dead and of the living.
ROMANS 14:7-9

What are two ways to demonstrate you live for yourself?

1.

2.

What are two ways to demonstrate you live for Christ?

1.

2.

How does knowing that Christ is Lord of both the living and the dead give you confidence to surrender to Him?

Jesus is Lord—He is the Master, Ruler, Final-Decision-Maker. And we belong to Him. Our identity as those who belong to the Lord becomes real to us as we become more submissive to Him. Our culture does not work this way. We are taught to work for our own power and control, but if we follow Jesus, we increasingly learn that someone else has already done all the work for us. Consider Paul's words:

For you have been bought with a price: therefore glorify God in your body.
1 CORINTHIANS 6:20

What right does Jesus's sacrifice on your behalf give Him over your life?

Jesus is to rule over our personal life, financial life, attitudinal life, relational life, and more. He reigns over it all because He owns it all. After all, He died for it all on the cross. If you want to see Jesus's rule on earth then you must allow Him to rule you from the heavenlies. He is better at controlling our lives than we are.

Are you living as an AM/FM Christian? What area
of your life are you withholding from Jesus?

Closing

As we close out this study, spend some time praying about your personal level of spiritual surrender. Identify areas where you need to improve and take the time to ask God to help you with that. If you feel fear or hesitation in surrendering to Jesus, then ask God to address those emotions as well. Jesus is Lord over all and He will meet you where you need Him most, but you do need to invite Him to carry out His will and His work within you.

BIBLE STUDY 2
Lord over All

What are some ways that our culture presses us
to consider ourself and our desires first?

When have you fallen victim to this cultural pressure?

You may think that you are taking care of yourself by focusing more on yourself than on Jesus and surrendering to His lordship over all. But in reality, you are shortchanging yourself. You are leaving the spiritual doors unlocked and the windows wide open so that Satan and circumstance can come in and steal from what God has provided for you.

As a result, you may wind up living under a cloud of spiritual theft, enabled through your own personal choices. You have given Satan the opportunity to sneak in and steal your joy. He has stolen your relationships. He has swiped your mental and emotional well-being and even your spiritual vitality. Worst of all, Satan may have even stolen your hope.

On a scale of 1-10 (with 10 being the most), where would you rate
your current level of hope for how things will turn out in your life?

1   10

What may have contributed to you choosing that number?

When you and I look around at the world, it is easy to lose hope. It is easy to do so because we allow cultural, social, political, racial, and economic factors to become the determining factor in our lives. As a result, we come up with all sorts of sociological explanations and labels and blame games for what has gone wrong.

Yet the reality is that everything we become entangled with or experience in the visible and physical world is preceded by that which is invisible and spiritual. Our problems have a spiritual cause. A spiritual root.

In order to address and correct the visible and physical reality we must identify the invisible and spiritual cause. Only when we identify and address the problem can we trace it back to it's root. As I've said many times, "If all you see is what you see, you do not see all there is to be seen."

If you only function in the realm of the five senses, then the enemy will be able to rip you off. In order to identify and reclaim that which is rightfully yours and embrace God's plan for your life, you must surrender to the lordship of Jesus Christ.

How does surrender develop our spiritual sensitivity?
How have you grown through surrender?

What area of your life do you most need to surrender to Jesus?

The wonderful thing about God is that He is always in control, whether we recognize it or not. As the psalmist says,

The LORD has established His throne in the heavens,
and His sovereignty rules over all.
PSALM 103:19

How does this verse bring you comfort?

God is in control even when things seem out of control. When you understand that He has the ultimate say over everything, it changes your priorities. When you recognize who sits on the throne above all politicians, celebrities, influencers, billionaires, and the like—it changes who you spend your time listening to, following, and seeking to align with. Jesus holds ultimate power and authority. Surrendering to Him is your greatest strategy for living the life He desires for you.

> List three thoughts or personal actions which cause you stress or worry and after you list them, ask Jesus to help you with all three. Commit to surrendering your thoughts and actions to Him and His will when you do.

1.

2.

3.

Satan's goal for believers is the same as it has always been. He wants to get us offtrack and unwilling to surrender to the lordship of Jesus Christ. Satan wants to take your purpose away from your life and experiences. The further he can get you or me offtrack, the more successful he is at accomplishing his goal.

Satan is relentless. He will seek to trip us up, accuse us, distract us, lull us to sleep, delight us into disobedience—any number of things. Yet despite his many tactics and methods, his goal remains the same—to strip us of our right to accessing the full kingdom authority God has available to us. When he does that, he reduces the advancement of God's kingdom agenda on earth through His followers.

> Where have you ceded your surrender so that you're actually giving the enemy a foothold into your life?

Why is trusting God and surrendering to Him a better
strategy than trying to climb your way out?

When we realize we're ensnared in one of Satan's traps, we tend to believe the way out is the way we got ourselves in—taking over for ourselves. The truth is that surrender is always the way out. Instead of surrendering to Satan and His schemes, we surrender to God, His rule, and His reign over our lives and our circumstances. As we do so, Christ and His rule are applied to our lives and we exercise the kingdom authority Christ provides to those who will take the key and surrender to Him.

Closing

Pray right now and ask Jesus to rule over your life—your thoughts,
words, desires, and actions. Ask Jesus to make His will known
to you more and more each day. Seek to find ways to honor
Jesus in all you say and do. Make His name known to others
throughout your normal, everyday experiences. As you incorporate
these prayers and actions into your life, you will witness His
power and authority more and more so on your behalf.

WEEK 5

PRAYER & KINGDOM AUTHORITY

Start

Welcome to group session 5.

What are some common reasons believers do not pray?

Why do you think it is so hard to live in a
posture of prayer towards God?

Prayer comes naturally to most of us, but prayer doesn't come naturally in every situation equally. We rarely think to pray about a mundane detail or a problem we believe we can handle on our own. We hold on to prayer as a last resort when it's clear that there is no path forward without it. Like we saw last session, the key to kingdom authority is surrender and it's available to us at all times. We just have to take it.

Praying in times of trouble seems natural to most of us. We can see the impossibilities in front of us and recognize we need God's help. But what we're going to look at in this week's study is how important prayer is to our everyday lives. We need to become more proactive to pray in the mundane and routine situations we face. God is God over all. He's given us access to kingdom authority for the big needs and the small.

Ask someone to pray then watch group session 5.

Watch

Take notes as you watch video session 5.

Discuss

Use the following questions to discuss the video teaching.

What is prayer? What do you believe is the purpose of prayer?

In the most basic definition, prayer is relational communication with God. It is the spiritual mechanism to connect our lives, spirits, and desires to God's will. Prayer doesn't mean we dictate to God what He is to do. Prayer is an action of aligning your heart and mind with God's will. God is not a vending machine where you insert some coins, push a few buttons, and get what you want. Prayer is more about what God wants than what we want.

Why do we have a tendency to treat prayer like a vending machine?

Share about a time when God did not answer your prayer as you had hoped, only to discover in hindsight that His answer was best.

Describe the relationship between trust, faith, and prayer.

Read Isaiah 55:8-11 then answer the following questions:

"For My thoughts are not your thoughts,
Neither are your ways My ways," declares the LORD.
"For as the heavens are higher than the earth,
So are My ways higher than your ways,
And My thoughts than your thoughts.
For as the rain and the snow come down from heaven,
And do not return there without watering the earth
And making it produce and sprout,
And providing seed to the sower and bread to the eater;
So will My word be which goes out of My mouth;
It will not return to Me empty,
Without accomplishing what I desire,
And without succeeding in the purpose for which I sent it.
ISAIAH 55:8-11

What does this passage teach us about God's desire
and ability to accomplish His kingdom agenda?

What does it tell us about our need to communicate with
Him to see His kingdom authority applied to us so that we
can partner with Him in accomplishing His agenda?

How does it take the pressure off of us to know that
God will accomplish His will regardless? In what
sense does that make prayer a privilege?

God's ways are not our ways and His thoughts are not our thoughts. We need to hear from Him and be in communion with Him to accomplish His will in our lives. This passage compares God's will to rain coming down from heaven watering the earth and producing that which God desires for it to produce. We are called to live in an ongoing mindset of prayer because prayer is critical to experiencing God's presence and provision in our lives. While it's easy to go to God in prayer in times of need or if we have a specific request, God desires that we recognize His hand and His will in all that takes place. When we begin to do that more readily, we get to experience what it means to walk in the Spirit and keep in step with His purpose for our lives.

Let's end our session in prayer.

Prayer

Lord, help us to pray more. Help us to understand how important
prayer is in relationship to kingdom authority. Open our eyes to see
Your hand involved in our lives so we can learn how to recognize more
of Your heart and more of Your work. Ignite our hearts and spirits with
a desire to communicate with You more. In Jesus's name, amen.

HIT THE STREETS

Pray Without Ceasing

All of us have spare tires in the trunks of our cars to use if we need them. Or, at least I hope you do. A spare tire was not created to be driven on for an extended period of time. It's designed to do the job until you can replace your damaged tire. The spare tire exists to bail you out of a bind.

Too many Christians view prayer like the spare tire in their trunk. It's there if you need it but it's not designed to go with you everywhere you go. It's not designed to be used for every mile of every moment in life. It's just there to bail you out of a bind.

However, 1 Thessalonians 5:17 says we are to "pray without ceasing." That sounds like a lot more than a spare tire to use in an emergency. To fully experience kingdom authority, you have to maintain relational communication with God. It's that straightforward. Use these three helpful tips to increase your prayer time and watch God show up in ways you've never experienced Him before.

1. When possible, journal your prayers. This may mean taking down notes of what you've prayed and dating it. It could be as extensive as writing your prayers out word for word. Whether you journal fully or simply take notes, the act of writing down what you are praying about will help you increase your engagement in prayer. It will also give you the opportunity to look back over your prayers and see how God has responded.

   How might this practice help build consistency in your prayer life?

2. Clear your schedule of clutter and noise. This action will help not only your prayer life but your whole life. One of Satan's primary strategies to keep us from spending time with God is distraction. A schedule full of unnecessary noise masks our need for God with the demands of daily life. Take time to examine your schedule and see what can be simplified.

> Off the top of your head, what is one activity or commitment
> that could be discarded to devote more time to prayer?

3. Pray about the small things. Even if it feels like it's too small for God to pay attention to—like getting a parking spot—go ahead and pray. As you turn to God in the smaller activities in your life, you will find it more meaningful and natural over time. Prayer will transition from something you "do" into more of a state of "being" as you make communication with God part of your everyday activities.

> What is a small thing you can pray about right now?

Prayer sits front and center in living out a life of kingdom authority. You must engage in prayer if you are to experience the power Christ has for you. Start incorporating these three things into your daily life as you grow in your walk with the Lord.

BIBLE STUDY 1

To Ask or Not to Ask

For many, prayer is like the announcements preceding an event.. It gets things going but doesn't seem to have anything to do with what's actually getting ready to take place—more ritual than relationship. Yet prayer, when fully understood, is authorized mechanism through which we draw heavenly authority down into our experience.

Prayer invites God's intervention into our experiences. When you fail to pray, it is as if you have turned off the reception on your phone in airplane mode. When you pray, you have powered it back up. James says that we do not have simply because we do not ask (James 4:2). In other words, when you don't pray, you also don't get what it is you are needing. This is true even though, depending on what it is, God has often already authorized that you could have it were you to ask for it.

Read the following Bible verses, summarizing the passage and writing down a personal application action item you learn from each one.

"If you remain in Me, and My words remain in you, ask whatever you wish, and it will be done for you."
JOHN 15:7

Summary:

Action Item:

"So I say to you, ask, and it will be given to you; seek, and you will find; knock, and it will be opened to you."
LUKE 11:9

Summary:

Action Item:

*"Call to Me and I will answer you, and I will tell you
great and mighty things, which you do not know."*
JEREMIAH 33:3

Summary:

Action Item:

"And whatever you ask in prayer, believing, you will receive it all."
MATTHEW 21:22

Summary:

Action Item:

---

*Now He was telling them a parable to show that at all times
they ought to pray and not become discouraged.*
LUKE 18:1

Summary:

Action Item:

Prayer is the mechanism through which you access kingdom authority. It is a dialogue with God which enables you to tap into all He has in store for you. I included just a few verses to respond to, but there are many more throughout Scripture that speak to this all-powerful form of communication with our Lord.

What we have to understand is when God created humanity, He uttered three words: "Let them rule" (Genesis 1:26). Those three words would be a defining mechanism and means for how God would interact and interface with planet earth and His creation. He gave us free will and the ability to participate in His governance.

Of course, the authority we've been given is supposed to be dependent upon God. When we rule in alignment under God, we have a vested interest to carry out kingdom rule on His behalf. But in order for us to do so well, we must maintain communication with Him. Rule has always been associated with relational intimacy with God. Adam and Eve walked with God. They interacted with God in the garden of Eden and communicated with Him. Rule and communication go hand in hand.

The chaos in our world today is a result of humanity's failure to rule well. Because so many people want to rule their lives, their homes, their families, their churches, their communities, and their civilizations independently of God's wisdom and truth, we find ourselves in a perpetual state of mayhem.

What is the difference between ruling under God's authority and ruling apart from God?

In what ways do we elevate our will and right to rule over God's sovereign rule in all creation?

Far too often people fall into two ditches related to prayer. Either they won't pray at all or when they do pray, they pray without an understanding that they are to get the direction for their prayers from heaven. To clarify how the concept of prayer works, I want to point out that God has both a conditional will and an unconditional will. God's conditional will involves those things that He will do only when certain conditions are met. God's unconditional will include those things God does without conditions attached to them. To be clear, all the promises God makes find there "yes" and "amen" in Christ (2 Corinthians 1:20), but there are blessings of God we miss out on by failing to pray or obey.

When it comes to God's conditional will, prayer is critical, because much of what God is doing we will miss or fail to be a part of because of our own stubornness and disobedience. He has instructed us to ask in order to receive.

We have also been told to abide in Christ in order to gain access to the things God has for us. These conditions have been put in place as part of the prayer process.

What are some blessings that God confers to
us through prayer and obedience?

Is there anything from God you are missing out on because of a
simple failure to communicate? If so, what? How will you correct it?

God has given us access to Himself through prayer. We have the choice on whether or not we want to participate in prayer like He has established. But if we choose not to participate according to His conditions, then we also relinquish a large portion, if not all, of our answers. Living with kingdom authority relies on a healthy and functional prayer life—a relationally-based communication process—with God Himself.

Closing

Take the remaining time in this study to pray to God. Praise Him for who He is. Ask Him for what You need. Request forgiveness from sins you have committed, and entrust yourself to His will and work in the world. Receive the blessing of prayer in faith with a glad and generous heart.

BIBLE STUDY 2

The Lord's Prayer

Who is the most consistent pray-er that you
know? What could you learn from them?

To take God for granted and not communicate the little things to Him is like the young boy who went to God over something seemingly small only to be told by an older relative, "I only take big things to God."

The young boy answered, "Well, I thought everything was little to God because God can handle anything." No matter what it is to us—big or small—it's always small to God. That's why He desires that we include Him in everything that we do. He is waiting to help us but He is often also waiting on us to invite Him into the situation—whether through asking for wisdom, intervention, or guidance.

The disciples were blessed with the opportunity to experience Jesus's prayer life on a number of occasions. They also got to see God respond to Christ's requests in prayer. Maybe that's why one of the disciples came to Jesus and asked Him to teach them to pray. We read this in Luke where it says,

> *It happened that while Jesus was praying in a certain place,*
> *when He had finished, one of His disciples said to Him, "Lord,*
> *teach us to pray, just as John also taught his disciples."*
> LUKE 11:1

Jesus accepted the invitation to teach them to pray and proceeded to give an example of what prayers should entail. We now call this example the "Lord's Prayer," and it goes like this:

> *"Father, hallowed be Your name.*
> *Your kingdom come.*
> *Give us each day our daily bread. And forgive us our sins,*
> *For we ourselves also forgive everyone who is indebted to us.*
> *And lead us not into temptation."*
> LUKE 11:2-4

Matthew records the Lord's Prayer like this:

"Our Father who is in heaven,
Hallowed be Your name.
Your kingdom come.
Your will be done,
On earth as it is in heaven.
Give us this day our daily bread. And forgive us our debts,
as we also have forgiven our debtors. And do not lead us
into temptation, but deliver us from evil. [For Yours is the
kingdom and the power and the glory forever. Amen.]"
MATTHEW 6:9-13 (NASB95)

Both Gospel writers captured Christ's prayer for us in order to demonstrate the importance of this act of communication with God. Prayer should never merely be relegated to just saying grace before a meal. As we can see by the example Jesus gave, our prayers are to cover a multiplicity of areas in order to fully witness God's hand of involvement in our lives.

What are some of the points of emphasis Jesus
gave us in His example of prayer?

Why is it important to view prayer as a comprehensive
communication strategy with God rather than a mere touch point?

Have you ever considered how you feel as you go through
your day when you intentionally pursue a more robust
prayer life with God? How does this compare to those times
when you merely "check in" with God here or there?

The Lord's Prayer serves as a model of how our prayers can be when we communicate with God. Briefly, it starts off with what I call the "**Paternity of Prayer**." This is where we address and acknowledge God as our Father. It also addresses where God abides. We've got a King who is in a heavenly kingdom and so we are to start our prayers giving Him the worship He is due.

Next, the example goes to what I call the "**Program of Prayer**." This is where we emphasize the main goal of God's kingdom rule manifested in history. As His followers, we are to be about the advancement of His kingdom agenda on earth. Praying to this end reminds us of this goal and helps bring it into reality. After this, we shift to the "**Priority of Prayer**." This involves recognizing and asking for God's will from heaven to be executed on earth.

Following this, we move to the "**Provision of Prayer**." By asking for our daily bread, we are reminded of our dependence on the King and His kingdom mechanisms in order to provide for us. All good things come from God. After this awareness and request, we move to the "**Pardon of Prayer**." This is an important aspect of prayer because sin puts static on the line so that our relationship with God is strained and feels distant. Anytime we have unaddressed sin in our lives, or even the failure to forgive others for what they have done to us, we are limiting our own effectiveness in prayer.

Going beyond forgiveness we reach the next part I call the "**Protection of Prayer**." This is where we pray for God to keep us from the tempter or the temptation that could ensnare us. Whenever we give in to temptation, it runs the risk of distracting us from God and derailing us from carrying out our kingdom purpose on earth. At the end of the prayer in Matthew, we then wind up with the "**Purpose of Prayer**." This is a reminder that the purpose is always about God and His kingdom. We are to speak, live, and pray in such a way that God's kingdom, power, and glory are made manifest throughout the world.

Take a moment to write out your thoughts and a
summary of each section of the Lord's Prayer and
how it can relate to your own prayer life.

Paternity of Prayer

Program of Prayer

Priority of Prayer

Provision of Prayer

Pardon of Prayer

Protection of Prayer

Purpose of Prayer

When Jesus gave His disciples an example of how to pray, He made sure to cover the various aspects which are so critical to living as a kingdom follower. Prayer isn't just about a meal or a request. It is to be first and foremost about the advancement of God's kingdom, as well as how to align yourself with the goals of that kingdom.

Let's close this session in prayer.

Closing

Jesus, I want to pray as You have shown me how to pray. I want to broaden my understanding of what prayer is to be about so that I can more effectively use it as a tool in my spiritual growth and development. Help me to understand Your example more clearly and help me to be more diligent to apply Your example to my personal prayer life. In Your name, amen.

WEEK 6

SCRIPTURE & KINGDOM AUTHORITY

Start

Welcome to group session 6.

We've come to our final session on kingdom authority. As a reminder, kingdom authority involves the right and the responsibility of believers to cooperate and act on God's behalf—in the rulership of His creation underneath the lordship of Jesus Christ. We've examined this important topic from several angles, and this week we will examine the importance of Scripture. You can't exercise kingdom authority without a right view of God's Word.

What are some of your favorite books to read or study in the Bible?

How has reading and studying God's Word helped
you know God and obey His commands?

The Word of God is living and authoritative. When it speaks, it speaks in finality. All of life is to be measured according to the authority of God's Word. Yet if we are going to exercise kingdom authority at the level that we can and should, we must allow God's Word to rightly govern all we think, say, and do.

Ask someone to pray then watch group session 6.

Watch

Take notes as you watch video session 6.

Discuss

Use the following questions to discuss the video teaching.

The final session for the *Kingdom Authority* study was filmed at a place called Muckross Abbey. This Abbey was founded in the mid-fifteenth century. As you can see by watching the video, much of it still stands, giving testimony to the strength of its walls.

The strength of this abbey's structure is a good illustration of how solid the Word of God is. It is authoritative. God's Word will not fall. It does not crumble. As Jesus puts it, "The Scripture cannot be broken" (John 10:35 NASB95).

What does it mean that Scripture cannot be
broken? What does it not mean?

How does that make Scripture different than
every other kind of book or writing?

In what ways does knowing that God's Word is authoritative
and unchanging bring you comfort and peace?

When Jesus said Scripture cannot be broken He was asserting that all of Scripture is enduring—it will always be true and authoritative—whether we acknowledge it or not. To reject the authority of Scripture is to reject Jesus Christ because the words of the Bible are His words. But when you understand that the Bible is the voice of God in print and has the final say on all areas of life, it will begin to change you.

Why is rejecting the authority and binding nature of
Scripture rejecting the authority of Jesus Christ?

Read 1 Thessalonians 2:13.

*For this reason we also constantly thank God that when you
received the word of God which you heard from us, you accepted
it not as the word of mere men, but as what it really is, the
word of God, which also is at work in you who believe.*
1 THESSALONIANS 2:13

How is the Word of God described in this passage?

What does it mean for the Word of God to
be "at work in you who believe"?

The Word of God is active and able to carry out God's work in your life. But you have to believe it and affirm it as authoritative and true in order to experience it. Problems arise when people choose to only hear the Word or maybe even read the Word but do not believe it to the point of welcoming it, embracing it, and acting on it. Their experience with it then becomes a document that is not activated authoritatively in their lives, for their benefit.

Give an example between hearing the Word and acting on the Word.

What results can you expect to see in your life if you reject the
authority of Jesus by rejecting the authority of the Word of God?

God's Word must be taken in and acted on before the authority of it is at work in your world. If we're going to be serious as believers in Jesus Christ and if we want to exercise the authority of eternity and draw it down into time, we have to start with Scripture. We have to apply its principles to our lives.

How will you engage with God's Word this week?

Let's close our last group session in prayer.

Prayer

Lord, we want to apply Your Word to our lives in all we do.
Give us an increased appetite for knowing and understanding
Your Word. Grow in our hearts the love we have for Your
Word. Help us to see the power of Your authority made
manifest in and through our lives. In Jesus's name, amen.

Benefiting from God's Word

Every situation in your life can benefit from shedding the light and truth of God's Word on it. It may seem difficult to locate a passage that speaks directly to the situation you are dealing with, but you can find passages that have principles which apply. It's important to look for the truth of the principles in the Word of God because these transcend time. As you apply biblical principles to your life, you will gain biblical wisdom that replaces and transcends the wisdom of this world.

To apply Biblical principles you must identify them. This requires dedicated time in the Word of God in order to observe and identify what God is saying throughout the biblical text. Use these three tips for how to create a meaningful Bible study time where you can gain a heart of wisdom from the Word.

1. Study the Scripture on a regular basis. Set aside time to simply read the Word every day. Whether you participate in a one-year Bible reading plan or choose to read through various books of the Bible, make your time consistent so that it becomes a habit.

   How can you make regular Bible reading a habit, if you haven't already?

2. Ask God to guide you as you read. Don't set out with your own agenda. Too often we go to the Word with the answer we are seeking to find already in our minds. We are looking for the Word of God to back a decision or thought we have. But learning from the Word means approaching the Word with an open heart and spirit and asking God to guide you.

   We studied prayer last week; how are prayer and Scripture reading intertwined and mutually beneficial practices?

3. There is a man in Scripture who knew he did not have enough faith. So he asked Jesus to give him more. Model this prayer when it comes to your hunger for the Word (Mark 9:24). Ask God to give you a greater hunger for knowing His Word. He will certainly answer this prayer if prayed sincerely because this prayer is in alignment with His will for your life.

How has God grown your faith in response to your request?
How does this help us understand how God works in our lives?

Growing your awareness and understanding of the Word of God will grow your spiritual muscles and faith. As you become a stronger follower of Jesus Christ, you will more naturally exercise kingdom authority as part of your normal routine. Make God's Word a priority and He will reveal to you your kingdom purpose as well as supply you with the authority and power to carry it out.

BIBLE STUDY 1

The Power of the Word

To begin today, consider this story. A college student had called his mom to let her know he was running out of money. He asked her to send him enough money to hold him over until his upcoming break. In a few days, he got a package from his mom. It wasn't an envelope like he expected. Rather, it was a Bible and a note. The note said, "Son, pray and read your Bible."

The young man called his mom obviously disappointed. "You know I love the Lord, mom," he said. "But I really need money right now. I'm about to run out."

His mom answered gently, "Son, just pray. And read your Bible." He could almost hear the smile on her face as she said it. But that just caused him to feel more disappointed. A few days later, he decided to call her again. "Mom," he said. "I'm completely out of money and it's not time for spring break."

To his chagrin, his mom replied exactly how he thought she would. "Son, pray. And read your Bible." This time she sounded more insistent. He still brushed her off. He didn't know how reading his Bible was going to help him get gas money. Eventually, he got mad. He borrowed some money from a friend and drove home. He was very upset and explained how he had a practical need but she just sent him the Bible. He had even brought the Bible with him as an illustration of how unpractically she had answered his request.

"Let me see your Bible," she said. So the son gave her the Bible. "Did you read it?" she asked. He nodded his head, although he wasn't telling the truth. His mom then opened the Bible and spread right there in the book of Psalms was five $100 bills. "You didn't read your Bible," she said. "Because if you had prayed and read your Bible, you would have understood that there is more in there than you could have ever imagined."

What God wants you to know is that there is more in His Word than you have ever imagined. The Bible isn't just to be held in your hand. It is to be experienced. It is to be lived out in your everyday life. The Bible points us to Christ.

Read 2 Peter 1:3.

For His divine power has granted to us everything pertaining
to life and godliness, through the true knowledge of Him
who called us by His own glory and excellence.
2 PETER 1:3

How does Christ make Himself known to us through the Bible?

According to Peter, what happens to us as we
receive Christ's power through the Word?

Jesus has granted us everything we need for life and godliness. These qualities come to us as we partake of Him through His Word. The Bible gives us the true knowledge of Jesus who called us by His glory and excellence. As we read the Scriptures, we are conformed to His image.

How has God guided you through His Word in the past?

What lessons did you learn from the times when
God used His Word to help you or show you which
way to go, or how to respond in a situation?

What does it mean to rely on God's Word in every area of life?

If we are going to be kingdom people exercising kingdom authority, then we're going to have to take seriously the fact that God's Word will always lead us to the truth. It provides an objective standard for a world that wants to look for truth everywhere else.

Truth is an absolute standard by which reality is measured. I know people talk about "my truth" and "their truth." But there's only *the* truth—God's Word. Whatever God says about a matter is the truth on the matter. It's the final statement on the subject. Only the Word of God can guide us to the truth.

Read Hebrews 4:12-13.

For the word of God is living and active, and sharper than any two-edged sword, even penetrating as far as the division of soul and spirit, of both joints and marrow, and able to judge the thoughts and intentions of the heart. And there is no creature hidden from His sight, but all things are open and laid bare to the eyes of Him to whom we must answer.
HEBREWS 4:12-13

What unique power does God's Word have in our lives?

God's Word is living and active. It isn't dead and static. God uses the Scripture to penetrate our hearts and make clear our intentions. Yet many of us seek truth outside of God's prescribed method for finding truth. No wisdom can ever replace God's wisdom through God's Word.

Why is it appealing, even for Christians, to find truth outside of God's Word?

What are some sources you or people you know
look to and embrace instead of the Bible?

Have you ever marginalized Scripture or the truth of
God's Word in your own life? What was the result?

Marginalizing God's Word in our lives marginalizes God in our lives. His Word provides what we need to know Him and obey His commands. It shapes us into people who represent Him and His rulership in the world. If we are going to be God's people exercising God's authority, His Word must be at the center of all we do because when Scripture is at the center, God is at the center. To deny the Word is to deny the power it brings.

It is in staying in alignment with the truth of God's Word that you access kingdom authority. If you were to mix a little bit of poison in with a lot of soup, the little bit of poison would ruin the entire soup. Yet today we don't seem to have any hesitation mixing worldly wisdom or worldly thought with the truth of God's Word. We do ourselves a disservice when we mix them, though, because we are stripping ourselves of the kingdom authority we need to fully live out God's call our on lives.

Closing

Pray and ask God to show you His truth more clearly through His Word. Ask Him to give you a hunger and thirst for the righteousness He makes known through the Scripture. Then be sure to set aside time each day to spend in God's Word getting to know Him as the author as well as His Word more fully.

BIBLE STUDY 2

Unscrambling the Word

There are twenty-six letters in the English alphabet. Any word you want to make must be made by arranging those twenty-six letters. It's a matter of arrangement. When my mom was alive, her absolute favorite game to play was Scrabble™. No matter how hard I tried, I could rarely beat my mom at Scrabble™. She had practiced over the years and turned into a master of the alphabet. She came up with words I had never even heard of!

For those of us who want to live with kingdom authority, we also have everything we need in the Bible. Just like every English word can be made from the twenty-six words in the alphabet, everything you and I need to exercise our faith and know God can be found in the Scriptures. To do that, we must understand and apply it to our unique situations.

When I was a kid, I loved watching *Soul Train*. On the show, they had what was known as a "Scramble Board" where letters to spell the song, album, or artist would be mixed up. Dancers would come over to the board and start putting letters back in order for the participants to guess until they formed the answer.

This game on *Soul Train* reminds me of our world. People are living scrambled lives. People's families are scrambled. Churches are scrambled. Society is scrambled. That's all because the Word of God is not in order. It's been mixed up and twisted by the world. It's only when we start to realign our lives to the truth of God's Word that life will make sense and we will know what we need to do.

If you and I are going to exercise the authority that is rightfully ours from up high in heaven in order to rule on God's behalf, we need to study it for ourselves and apply it. But we also need to make it our effort to share the truth of God with those around us.

How are you putting the Word of God into your heart and mind?

What are some ways you can share what
God is teaching you with others?

Why is it important to apply God's Word once we
understand it? How can we help others do the same?

There are so many version of the truth these days that it's hard to know which way is up. What we need more than ever are people who will lovingly and compassionately share the truth of God's Word with others. We need followers of Jesus Christ to no longer be ashamed of the gospel or the Scriptures.

Why might we be ashamed of the gospel and the Scriptures?

How does being ashamed of the Scriptures keep you
from experiencing what they have to offer?

In the video this week, we talked about the old Negro baseball league umpire, Bill Klem. In the last inning of of a tie game, the batter hit a ground ball which was fielded by the second baseman. The second baseman threw the ball to the catcher to stop the runner at home from walking off with the game-winning run.

But when the runner crossed the plate, there was so much dust in the air that no one could tell what had happened. All eyes went to Klem. He had given the sign but no one had seen it through the dust. Both benches emptied out to argue their point to the umpire. Yet in the midst of the chaos, the umpire shouted, "Quiet! Quiet! Because it's nothing other than what I've called!"

No argument needed to take place. The umpire had made the call and that call would stand. Similarly, we have a lot of division and arguing going on in our society and world today. Everyone seems to have an argument. Everyone seems to have a voice. And everyone seems to be just getting louder with time. But Jesus Christ has told us what the call is. He's told us what the answers are. And He's got His hand up to let us know that He's in charge. All of the issues we are divided on are nothing other than what He's called in the Word of God.

What are some ways division keeps us from
learning and living the truth of God?

Which of our arguments would subside if we simply pressed into
the Word of God rather than our arguments with each other?

What are you missing in your life because you're
arguing your way over God's call?

How does division and diversion make us ineffective kingdom disciples?

We're all on a journey of growing in Christ. But that journey must be based on the firm foundation of the Word of God. It's hard to hear and understand God's Word if we are so caught up in the arguments taking place on the field of life. It's only when we prioritize the Word of God and the truth of God that we will see order return to our personal lives, families, churches, communities, society, and our world.

List a few takeaways from your time studying kingdom authority.

Where does the Lord most need you to go out and exercise the kingdom authority He has given you?

Let's close our time together in this Bible study with prayer.

Closing

Pray as you feel led to do so and as you do, remember the things we have covered together. Ask God to work on you in the areas where you need work, and to affirm in you the areas you are doing well and need to share with others so that they will also grow. Together, we can raise up a stronger, more unified body of believers who can influence our culture for good by tapping into and unleashing the kingdom authority God has provided to us through Christ Jesus.

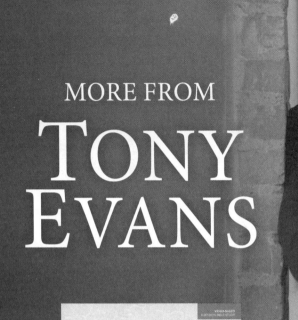

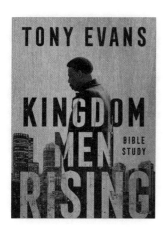

KINGDOM MEN RISING
Heaven's Representatives on Earth

Discover the biblical truth about the purpose and future of masculinity, and inspire your group to fulfill God's intent. (6 sessions)

Bible Study Kit $99.99
Bible Study Book $14.99

U-TURNS
Reversing the Consequences in Your Life

Learn to align your life choices under God's Word and change the direction of your life. (6 sessions)

Bible Study Kit $99.99
Bible Study Book $14.99

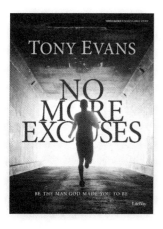

NO MORE EXCUSES
Be the Man God Made You to Be

Learn to lay down your excuses, stop compromising, and fight to be a man of character and commitment. (8 sessions)

Bible Study Kit $99.99
Bible Study Book $14.99

YOUR *Eternity* IS OUR *Priority*

At The Urban Alternative, eternity is our priority—for the individual, the family, the church and the nation. The 45-year teaching ministry of Tony Evans has allowed us to reach a world in need with:

The Alternative – Our flagship radio program brings hope and comfort to an audience of millions on over 1,300 radio outlets across the country.

tonyevans.org – Our library of teaching resources provides solid Bible teaching through the inspirational books and sermons of Tony Evans.

Tony Evans Training Center – Experience the adventure of God's Word with our online classroom, providing at-your-own-pace courses for your PC or mobile device.

Tony Evans app – Packed with audio and video clips, devotionals, Scripture readings and dozens of other tools, the mobile app provides inspiration on-the-go.

**Explore God's kingdom today.
Live for more than the moment.
Live for** *eternity.*

tonyevans.org

Accept God's rule and leadership in your life.

Are you ready to fight against the forces of darkness by exercising the delegate authority you have from God as a follower of Jesus?

In this study you'll:

- Learn to live under God's authority
- Overcome the strategies and schemes of the devil through God's power
- Cease being overwhelmed by circumstances and embrace God's leadership

STUDYING ON YOUR OWN?

To enrich your study experience, be sure to access the videos available through a redemption code printed in this *Bible Study Book.*

LEADING A GROUP?

Each group member will need a *Kingdom Authority Bible Study Book,* which includes video access. Because all participants will have access to the video content, you can choose to watch the videos outside of your group meeting if desired. Or, if you're watching together and someone misses a group meeting, they'll have the flexibility to catch up!

KINGDOM AUTHORITY

LIVING UNDER GOD'S RULE

TONY EVANS

Here's Your Video Access

To stream the Bible study teaching videos, follow these steps:

1. Go to my.lifeway.com/redeem and register or log in to your Lifeway account.

2. Enter this redemption code to gain access to your individual-use video license:

2 Z D Q M A M N W Z

Once you've entered your personal redemption code, you can stream the Bible study teaching videos any time from your Digital Media page on my.lifeway.com or watch them via the Lifeway On Demand app on a compatible TV or mobile device via your Lifeway account.

There's no need to enter your code more than once!
To watch your streaming videos, just log in to your Lifeway account at my.lifeway.com or watch using the Lifeway On Demand app.

QUESTIONS? WE HAVE ANSWERS!
Visit support.lifeway.com and search "Video Redemption Code" or "Video Streaming FAQ" or call our Tech Support Team at 866.627.8553.